Contents

Breakfast is cooking . . . Say what you see!

frying

Say What You See

Eat

Rebecca Rissman

Raintree

Chicago, Illinois

Edited by Rebecca Rissman, Daniel Nunn, and Catherine Veitch
Designed by Philippa Jenkins
Picture research by Ruth Blair
Production by Victoria Fitzgerald
Originated by Capstone Global Library
Printed and bound in the United States of America in
North Mankato, Minnesota.

072016
009883RP

Library of Congress Cataloging-in-Publication Data
Rissman, Rebecca.
Eat / Rebecca Rissman.
p. cm.—(Say What You See)
Includes bibliographical references and index.
ISBN 978-1-4109-5047-5 (hb)—ISBN 978-1-4109-5052-9 (pb)—
1. Food—Juvenile literature. 2. Cooking—Juvenile literature. I.
Title.
TX355.R537 2013
641.3—dc23   2012011708

Acknowledgments
We would like to thank the following for permission to reproduce
photographs: Shutterstock pp. title page (© ravl), 4 (© Nattika),
5 (© Charlotte Lake, © Petr Malyshev, © Bratwustle), 6 (©
Ieva Vincer), 7 (© Petro Feketa, © Analia Valeria Urani), 8 (©
discpicture), 9 (© trevorb), 10 (© Gunnar Pippel, © Monkey
Business Images), 12 (© 3445128471), 13 (© .shock, © corepics),
15 (© Africa Studio, © Jiri Hera), 16 (© JohanKalen), 17 (© Andrey
Armyagov, © Firma V), 18 (© ssuaphotos), 19 (© T-3, © .shock,
© oknoart), 20 (© Rob Marmion), 21 (© MikLav, © Gorilla), 22 (©
Monkey Business Images); Superstock pp. 9 (© Flirt), 11 (© Blend
Images), 13 (© Fancy Collection), 14 (© Corbis), 15 (© BlueMoon
Stock).

Cover photograph of a girl taking a bite out of a watermelon
reproduced with permission of iStockphoto (© Kim Gunkel).

Every effort has been made to contact copyright holders of
material reproduced in this book. Any omissions will be rectified
in subsequent printings if notice is given to the publisher.

stirring

Pouring

flipping

peeling

Baking

whisking

Boiling

Scrambling

It's nearly time for lunch . . .
Say what you see!

Crunching

Slurping

Slurping

Slicing

Grilling

Blending

Tossing

Scooping

Dipping

Spreading

Chopping

It's dinner time . . .
Say what you see!

Twisting

Chewing

Cutting

Roasting

Rising

Melting

Steaming

Eating gives us energy for . . .

growing!

Playing!

Thinking!

We eat to be healthy . . .
and because food tastes great!

Can you find these things in the book? Look back . . . and say what you see!

stirring

slicing

crunching

melting

Index

Eat

TOASTING   Roasting   **Boiling**

It's time to eat!

Children will love looking at the photographs and learning new words in this simple label book. Enjoy teaching children new vocabulary as they explore a world of food and drinks and learn to say what they see!

Titles in the **Say What You See** series:

Animals
Eat
Family
Play

Heinemann Raintree

a capstone imprint   www.capstonepub.com

Language Arts

ISBN 978-1-4109-5052-9

90000

9 781410 950529

Animals